The Jamestown Church
Jamestown, VA

D1451664

HISTORIC
Jamestowne®
AMERICA'S BIRTHPLACE

About Historic Jamestowne

Historic Jamestowne is jointly administered by APVA Preservation Virginia and the National Park Service in order to preserve, protect, and interpret the original site of the first permanent English settlement in North America to the public. Through museum exhibits, tours, and the landscape itself, Historic Jamestowne tells the story of the three cultures—European, North American, and African—that came together to lay the foundation for uniquely American forms of democratic government, language, free enterprise, and society.

About APVA Preservation Virginia

APVA Preservation Virginia was founded in 1889 in order to preserve some of Virginia's most significant landmarks, including Jamestown. Since its inception, the efforts of the APVA have been instrumental in preserving more than 120 historic sites across Virginia, representing four centuries of American history. Today the APVA is the oldest statewide preservation organization in the United States with a mission to preserve and protect, as well as educate. A wide variety of programs fulfill this mission.

The Jamestown Church was produced by Dementi Milestone Publishing in collaboration with the Staff of APVA Preservation Virginia.

Written by: Lou Ann Meadows Ladin with Catherine Dean and Dia Idleman

Photography by: Wayne Dementi and Gene Payne. Additional images from the APVA Preservation Virginia archives and sources noted in captions.

Design by: Dot Anderson, Anderson Advertising/Graphics, Inc., Richmond, Virginia

Inside front cover: "Site of Jamestown," nineteenth-century engraving: F.B Schell—designer, H.S. Beckwith—engraver, Transferred to glass and painted with oil colors by John J. Carow.
APVA Preservation Virginia collection

All distribution rights belong to APVA Preservation Virginia

ISBN 0-9773153-3-9

Copyright 2007 by APVA Preservation Virginia

Published by Dementi Milestone Publishing, Richmond, Virginia

Table of Contents

The phrase "white gloves and red bricks" has come to symbolize the ladies who founded and built the Association for the Preservation of Virginia Antiquities. These ladies are attending the church service held during the visit of Queen Elizabeth II to Virginia in 1957.

Introduction

by Elizabeth Kostelny, Executive Director APVA Preservation Virginia

Sifting through the rubble in 1897, Miss Mary Jeffery Galt and her fellow "archae-ologists" came face-to-face with the history of this nation. They understood that standing where history happened sends a powerful message. That message has been a draw throughout the years as presidents, heads of state, queens, kings, and everyday folks travel to Historic Jamestowne and, in particular, the site of the 1617 church.

Churches occupy a unique place in American society. Places of worship, expressions of spiritual values, and identity come to mind first. Churches are central to the community—the social interaction where friends and acquaintances catch up on daily life and significant events. Before the defined line between church and state was drawn, places of worship had governmental functions.

Churches are also places of grounding, centering, and renewing. The truth in that statement was brought home to us all at Historic Jamestowne in September 2001. After the tragic events of 9/11, visitors to the area and neighbors alike flocked to the Jamestown Memorial Church to contemplate the events and to honor the victims. People gathered for comfort, strength, and resolve from a place that bore witness to the enduring qualities of our American way of life. The Jamestown Church remains that enduring and hallowed place.

When first established, the Jamestown Church was a center not only for the people of Jamestown, but also for those in outlying plantations and communities that traveled to worship. In 1619 with the convening of the first legislative assembly, the role of this structure took on a new dimension and significance. Unknowingly, the individuals called to govern set off a series of events that forever changed the world and planted the seeds of democracy.

The capital's move to Williamsburg in 1699 slowed life at Jamestown. Eventually, the Church became a symbol rather than a community center. Abandoned and falling into disrepair, the walls of the Church crumbled, leaving only its tower standing as a sentinel guarding the sacred site. By the early nineteenth century, artists squarely within the Romantic Movement were moved to paint compositions of the natural forces and their interplay on the structure of the Church. Its transcendental qualities captured the essence of nature and history at once intertwined.

Years passed. Throughout the nineteenth century, the church tower and the adjoining graveyard attracted individuals and groups to the hallowed ground to honor events and people—and inspiration struck again!

In 1889, confronted by an ever-growing inventory of noteworthy yet deteriorating historic places, including Powhatan's Chimney, the Powder Magazine in Williamsburg, and the Jamestown church tower, a group of women came together to found the Association for the Preservation of Virginia Antiquities, the first organization of its kind. Organized as a statewide preservation organization, this newly formed group was intent on acquiring and preserving significant historic landmarks and advocating for the preservation of the structural symbols of our past. Jamestown became a catalyst for another first.

While grassroots organizations are the norm today, these movements were rare during the turn of the twentieth century. The women launched a movement that valued place as a way to remember and to learn from our past. To save Jamestown, they enlisted friends and family to negotiate a complicated deal that ultimately became a substantial gift of twenty-two acres of Jamestown Island in 1893. The work had only begun.

Mary Jeffery Galt, her sister, Annie, and Miss Mary Garrett began to excavate the foundations of the church to rediscover the history through this site. They preserved the discoveries they found among the ruins. By securing the assistance of the Army Corps of Engineers, construction of a seawall began ensuring the church tower's safety from threat of the lapping James River. The generosity of the National Society of the Colonial Dames of America made possible the construction of a Memorial Church to straddle and preserve the 1617 and 1639 foundations. The Jamestown Church again stood ready to teach lessons to future generations so that they might learn from the past.

Descriptions, paintings, and photographs chronicle the Jamestown Church throughout the centuries. As the most lasting symbol of this place, the church possesses power, and its profound influence remains clear. Whether it is through John Pory's description about the gathering of the first Assembly or the look of longing on Shirley Carter's face in the circa 1890 photograph, each reveals events that transpired at this place that changed the world forever.

Today as before, the Jamestown Memorial Church stands as a testament to the enduring qualities of American society. Inspiring the divine and the preservation-minded, Historic Jamestowne remains hallowed ground.

Photo of the church tower from about 1890.
The man in the foreground is believed to be
Mr. Shirley Carter of Shirley Plantation.

Wee did hang an awning (which is an old saile) to three or foure trees to shadow us from the Sunne, our walls were rales of wood, our seats unhewed trees, till we cut plankes, our Pulpit a bar of wood nailed to tow neighbouring trees, in foule weather we shifted into an old rotten tent.

–Captain John Smith

Chapter One
The History of the Jamestown Church

In the heart of Historic Jamestowne stands the Memorial Church, built over the actual foundations of the Jamestown Church of 1617 and itself an iconic symbol of the foundation of both Christianity and representative government in America. To fully appreciate the significance of the Memorial Church, it is helpful to first understand how Jamestown began.

On May 13, 1607, three ships—the Susan Constant, the Discovery and the Godspeed—set anchor in the tidal floodwaters of the James River. The more than one hundred men and boys aboard the ships had spent the past five months first crossing the Atlantic Ocean and then exploring the Virginia coast in search of a perfect site to build their settlement. The colony they built would come to be known as Jamestown. It would be the first permanent English settlement in North America and play an important role in the establishment of representative government and the Protestant religion in North America.

The Jamestown settlers had been sent by a group of investors in England called the Virginia Company of London. The Company was formed with the intention of making

profit for its backers and was granted permission to establish a new colony in Virginia by England's King James I. If the colony was successful and produced profitable goods, the partners would earn money. If it failed, they would lose their investment. The Virginia Company appointed leaders for the fledgling colony and provided instructions on where they should settle and how they should establish themselves in the new land.

The first English settlers in Jamestown had many reasons for moving so far from home. Many wanted to own land and gain riches; others wanted a chance to see new worlds. Some of the colonists wanted to bring their religious ideas to the Virginia Indians and convert them to Christianity.

Formalized religion played a role in the lives of the Jamestown settlers from the very beginning. When they first landed on Virginia soil, at nearby Cape Henry, they are said to have fallen to their knees and said a prayer, thanking God for their safe arrival. They erected a makeshift cross at the site before sailing up the James River in search of a settlement site.

At Jamestown, the initial worship services of the new colony took place in the forest

The National Society of the Daughters of the American Colonists erected a granite cross near the site of the first landing at Cape Henry to commemorate the first landing of the Jamestown colonists.

beneath a tattered sailcloth hung between a few trees. Captain John Smith described it in his journal:

> *Wee did hang an awning (which is an old saile) to three or foure trees to shadow us from the Sunne, our walls were rales of wood, our seats unhewed trees, till we cut plankes, our Pulpit a bar of wood nailed to tow neighbouring trees, in foule weather we shifted into an old rotten tent.*

Bronze bas relief from the Hunt Shrine depicting the first Holy Communion by the settlers in 1607.

Reverend Robert Hunt

Richard Hakluyt, prebendary of Westminster, was an enthusiast for colonial expansion. He had done much to interest James I in the Virginia Company's undertaking. Hakluyt was honored by appointment as rector of the Jamestown parish. But he was an aging scholar, and not up to the arduous journey. In his stead, he chose Reverend Robert Hunt as his vicar at Jamestown.

It was Robert Hunt who presided over the first Anglican service in Jamestown and took his place in history. The humble setting was a far cry from the grand edifices of the churches in England, but the colonists' faith was not diluted by their primitive environs.

Reverend Robert Hunt, the first minister of America's first Anglican church at Jamestown, holds a special place in the history of the colony. He was not only the religious leader of his congregation, but a secular leader as well. As such, he bore the additional duties of keeping basic government records, helping maintain order in the community and disseminating information to the parishioners. His sermons would have discussed theology, along with morality, politics and current affairs.

The Reverend Robert Hunt Shrine at Historic Jamestowne.

Captain John Smith relates a story of Reverend Hunt's skill as a mediator. He wrote of a dispute between himself and the Council, "the good doctrine and exhortation of our preacher Master Hunt reconciled them and caused Captaine Smith to be admitted to Councell; the next day all received the Communion."

Reverend Hunt was greatly admired by the members of the colony. John Smith left this testimony describing him:

> He was an honest, religious and courageous divine, he preferred the service of God in so good a voyage to every thought of ease at home. He endured every privation, yet none ever heard him repine [complain]. During his life our factions were oft healed and our greatest extremities so comforted that they seemed easy in comparison with what we endured after his memorable death. We all received from him the Holy Communion together as a pledge of reconciliation for we all loved him for his exceeding goodness. He planted the first Protestant church in America, and laid down his life in the foundation of Virginia.

In 1922, the Virginia Chapter of the National Society of the Colonial Dames of America erected a shrine in honor of Reverend Robert Hunt at Jamestown. The memorial depicts the first celebration of Holy Communion by the settlers in 1607. A bronze tablet framed by two 16-foot high brick pillars and a sandstone arch, depicts that historic service. Ralph Adams Cram designed the memorial. The Colonial Dames said of architect Cram that, "due to his ecclesiastical genius that a shrine to the glory of God and in memory of Robert Hunt, with communion rail and table of stone stands in exquisite reverence and simplicity in Jamestown today."

The Hunt Shrine still stands at Historic Jamestowne today. Visitors can find it along the waterfront between the 1607 fort site and the Archaearium.

This image shows a digital model of the James Fort circa 1607–1624 superimposed on a modern aerial view of Historic Jamestowne. The darker buildings represent structures located during archaeological excavations. The ghosted buildings and features are based on archaeologists' best guesses of what may have been in areas of the fort that have not been excavated thoroughly as of 2006.

Locating the Site of the First Church

Debate continues today over the exact location of the first church. Some believe that once the first church was built, no matter how rustic, it would have been consecrated ground and the settlers would not have chosen a new location for later, more permanent structures. As the Jamestown Rediscovery® team began their search for the site of the original settlement, they began with the assumption that the seventeenth-century church tower still standing today, would have been the location for the first church and that the church would have been located near the center of the fort, as in the 1993 and 1994 predictive models. However, excavations have determined the location and shape of the 1607 fort to be somewhat different than initially expected. The Memorial Church that stands at Historic Jamestowne today was built in 1907 over the 1617 foundations. It is located just outside of the palisade walls of 1607, but inside the area of a later fort expansion. Archaeologists still hope to find evidence of the first church within the outline the 1607 fort as excavations continue.

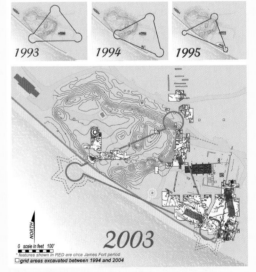

Initially Jamestown Rediscovery® archae-ologists believed that the church stood within the footprint of the original 1607 James Fort. Later excavations revealed that the church was actually just outside of its boundaries.

4

This portrait of John Smith is based on a seventeenth-century engraving.

The settlers replaced the makeshift shelter with a wooden church during the summer of 1607. It is believed to have stood within the safe confines of the fort the settlers had constructed soon after landing but archaeological evidence of the exact location of this church has not yet been discovered. Captain Smith described the first Anglican church in Virginia as "a homely thing like a barne, set upon cratchets, covered with rafts, sedge and earth."

Such were the beginnings of the first Protestant church in the brave new world known as America.

This rustic wooden church served as the site of funeral services for the 60 men and boys who died during the first few months of the fledgling community. The mortality rate among the first Jamestown settlers was staggering. These colonists who had voyaged to America for "God, Gold and Glory," were struck down by famine, disease and attacks by the Virginia Indians defending their land. John Smith wrote of the first summer that "the living were scarcely able to bury the dead."

However, the church did not last long. It burned in the great fire of January 1608, which destroyed much of the fort. The determined colonists built a new frame church when they rebuilt the fort, their houses and other communal buildings. The second church was said to be similar in appearance to the first: 60 feet by 24 feet with a steeple at its west end.

The seal of the Virginia Company of London.

This style of church was known as a "room" or "auditory" church, popular in the early seventeenth century. It had no structural differentiation between the chancel (the space around the altar) and the nave (the longitudinal area of a church that runs from the main entrance to the chancel). Medieval churches typically housed the chancel in a separate wing. In the room church, the chancel and nave may have been separated only by a screen.

The second church would stand somewhat longer and achieve historical significance as the site of the first Anglican wedding in Virginia. In 1609 John Laydon married Anne Burras, one of the first two women to come to Jamestown. A year later, the church was the site of the first baptism in the settlement when their daughter, Virginia Laydon, was christened.

The second Jamestown Church evidently deteriorated after a few years and was said to have been abandoned prior to 1617 when Captain Samuel Argall became Governor. When Argall came to Jamestown, he reportedly found:

> *but five or six houses, the church downe, the palizados (palisades) broken, the bridge in pieces, the well of fresh water spoiled, the storehouse used for the church; the marketplace, the streets and all other spare places planted with tobacco; the savages as frequent in their homes as themselves, whereby they were become expert in our armes... the Colonie dispersed all about planting Tobacco.*

Today the original cobblestone foundations of the 1617 church are visible under glass in the Jamestown Memorial Church.

It has been speculated that Argall chose to move the church site to a new location. The boundaries of the original fort were expanding eastward as the settlement grew and it was in this expansion area that the new church was built. He ordered the building of a frame structure slightly smaller than the previous church, measuring 50 feet long and 20 feet broad. The third church was built on a foundation of cobblestones one foot wide capped by a wall one brick thick. These very foundations are visible under the glass on the floor of the Jamestown Memorial Church.

This third church at Jamestown would become one of the most important buildings in American history. Within its walls, the first representative legislative assembly in America would meet in 1619.

A close up view of the original foundations of the church, thought to date to 1617.

Prior to the creation of the representative assembly, Virginia was governed by the "Lawes Divine, Morall and Martiall," a form of martial law. The colonists were instructed by the Virginia Company "to establish one and uniform government over all Virginia" which would provide "just laws for the happy guiding and governing of the people there inhabiting." The representative Assembly replaced this martial government but enacted numerous laws similar to those previously in effect.

On Friday July 30, 1619, the General Assembly met for the first time, in response to the orders of the Virginia Company. It consisted of the Governor, the Council of Estate, and the House of Burgesses. The Council consisted of men selected by the Virginia Company while the House of Burgesses consisted of two representatives democratically elected from each settlement in Virginia.

The members of the first General Assembly were:

Governor: Sir George Yeardley.

Council: Mr. Samuel Macock, Mr. John Rolfe, Mr. John Pory, Captain Nathaniel Powell, Captain Francis West, Reverend William Wickham.

House of Burgesses: For James City: Captain William Powell and Ensign William Spense; for Charles City: Samuel Sharpe and Samuel Jordan; for the City of Henricus: Thomas Dowse and John Polentine; for Kiccowtan: Captain William Tucker and William Capp; for Martin-Brandon, Captain John Martin's Plantation: Thomas Davis and Robert Stacy; for Smythe's Hundred: Captain Thomas Graves and Walter Shelley; for Martin's Hundred: John Boys and John Jackson; for Argall's Gift: Thomas Pawlett and Edward Gourgainy; for Flowerdew Hundred: Ensign Edmund

This painting, created by Virginia artist Sidney King around 1957, depicts the first meeting of the first House of Burgesses at the Jamestown Church.
APVA Preservation Virginia collection

Rossingham and John Jefferson; for Captain Lawne's Plantation: Captain Christophor Lawne and Ensign Washer; for Captain Warde's Plantation: Captain John Warde and Lieutenant John Gibbes.

John Pory, a member of the Council and Secretary of the Colony, noted that "the most convenient place we could finde to sitt was the Quire of the churche." The men took their seats, a prayer was said by Minister Bucke and the session got underway. The Assembly conducted its business in heat so extreme that one Burgess died during the session. When the legislature adjourned on August 4, 1619, its members had framed six petitions to the Virginia Company, considered four petitions, sat as a court on two occasions, raised enough taxes to pay for the session and passed 38 laws.

These laws forbid such transgressions as idleness, gaming, swearing and drunkenness and gave the minister the authority to excommunicate parishioners who did not comply with church authority. The emphasis on moral law was intended to encourage proper conduct for the individual, but in the larger sense preserve order and harmony within the settlement.

By 1629, some government meetings were taking place in the "Statehouse," which was the residence of the Royal Governor of Virginia, Sir John Harvey. However, the Virginia Assembly probably continued to meet at the Jamestown Church past that date, and possibly until construction of the new brick church began sometime around 1639. Regardless of exactly how long the Virginia Assembly met in the Jamestown Church, those meetings left a permanent legacy, which laid the foundation for America's elective, democratic, bi-cameral (having two legislative chambers) form of government.

The third church endured for about 20 years or so, and was then replaced by a brick structure. The fourth church, long thought to have been built in 1639, was more likely built in the 1640s or early 1650s. It was somewhat larger than the third church and was built on the same site. Brick was used for the first time in constructing this church, probably in response to a 1639 ordinance that required new construction to be made of brick, rather than wood, to reduce the threat of fire and give the settlement a more permanent appearance.

The brick church was built with funds from Governor John Harvey and other wealthy colonists. Harvey wrote: "Such hath our Indeavour herein, that out of our owne purses wee have largely

The House of Burgesses Monument

The House of Burgesses monument stands within the 1607 fort site at Historic Jamestowne. It was erected by the Norfolk branch of the APVA in 1907 to commemorate the first representative legislative body in America.

The inscription on the side of the monument facing the Jamestown Church reads:

In Honour of the First General Assembly of Virginia. Here on the thirtieth day of July A.D. 1619 summoned by Sir George Yeardley, Governor General of Virginia under authority from the London Company pursuant to the charter granted by King James I, was convened in the church at Jamestown the first General Assembly of Virginia.

This Assembly composed of the Governor, the Council of State and two Burgesses elected by the people from each of eleven plantations was the beginning of representative government in the colonies of England and laid the foundation of the liberties of America.

On the opposite side of the monument are the names of the Burgesses who represented settlements on the James River.

contributed to the building of a brick church, and both Masters of Shippe and the others of the ablest Planters have liberally by our persuasion underwritt to this worke."

The fourth church became the official church for the Governor, the House of Burgesses and members of the judiciary. It remained in use for several decades until it was burned down on September 19, 1676 by Nathaniel Bacon and his rebels. Following the fire the church was rebuilt on the same spot, likely using the remaining walls and foundations, sometime before the early 1680s. This fifth church is said to have served as the model for Bruton Parish Church in Williamsburg, which was probably built in the 1680s.

Bishop Meade measured the foundations on a visit to Jamestown sometime before 1856. He noted that the plan of the church was that of a basilica. The dimensions of the fifth and last church were 28 feet by 56 feet, according to Bishop Meade. The tower was

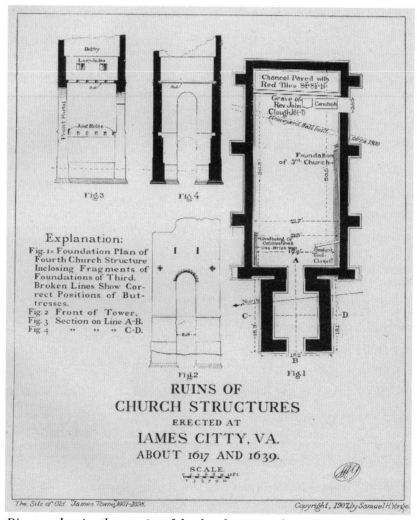

Diagram showing the remains of the church ruins at the Jamestown Memorial Church site as documented by Samuel H. Yonge in his 1907 book The Site of Old "James Towne," *1607–1698.*

One of the earliest known photographs of the Church Tower, said to date from 1883, taken by J. T. Rothrock.

about 46 feet high (ten feet higher than it stands today) and was crowned with a wooden roof and belfry. It had two upper floors as indicated from the large beam notches on the inside. The topmost floor may have been used as a lookout post. Six small openings at the top of the tower permitted light to enter and the sound of the bell or bells to carry across river and town. The tower was slightly over 18 feet square and the walls three feet thick at the base.

The previous school of thought held that the tower was constructed around 1639. Recent research, however, indicates that it was probably added sometime in the 1690s. This later date would correspond to the time that the Reverend James Blair, the Bishop of London's Commissary for Virginia, was in residence at Jamestown. In 1699, the church wardens reportedly petitioned the Virginia Assembly for funds "towards the paying for the Steeple of their Church, and towards the Repairing of the Church." Furthermore, architectural research points out that the type of brickwork makes it unlikely that the tower was built prior to Bacon's Rebellion. Additionally, certain features of the tower, such as its compass-headed windows, did not appear in Virginia until the last quarter of the seventeenth century.

Watercolor illustration of ruins of the Jamestown Church from Amoenitates Graphicae *by Louis Girardin, Williamsburg , 1805.*
Special Collections, John D. Rockefeller, Jr Library. The Colonial Williamsburg Foundation

The fifth and final church was used until the 1750s when it was abandoned due to a decline in population at Jamestown. By then the capital of Virginia had moved to Williamsburg and the land at Jamestown was used primarily as farmland. Eventually only two families, the Amblers and the Travises, remained on the island.

The church tower, or portions thereof, stood resolutely against the ravages of time. However, the building had fallen into ruins by the end of the eighteenth century. Bricks from the crumbled walls were used to enclose part of the graveyard. The ruins were a forlorn sight, described by a diarist

A modern day view of the church graveyard. The wall surrounding it is made of bricks salvaged from the ruins of the church that was abandoned in the 1750s.

in 1777 who lamented that "tall trees grow in the churchyard which serve as haunt for blackbirds and crows, and add to the Gloom of the Prospect." It was a sad setting for the only remaining evidence of the seventeenth-century colonial capital of Virginia.

There was sporadic activity at Jamestown over the years. It was fortified during the Revolutionary War of 1776 and the War of 1812. During the Civil War in 1861, General Robert E. Lee built several earthen fortifications, the primary one being Fort Pocahontas near the old church tower. Later archaeological excavations would reveal that the Confederate fort was built on top of part of the 1607 James Fort.

After the Civil War, a succession of farmers owned the island. The church ruins, tower and graveyard, though viewed sympathetically by the public, stood unprotected and were often scavenged by relic hunters. Ownership of the church property eventually reverted to the State of Virginia. However, change was astir. The dawning realization that many irreplaceable historic landmarks and objects were being lost for posterity was spreading across the country. A new sense of preservationism was taking root and nowhere would this be more important than in Virginia, the birthplace of the nation.

This nineteenth-century engraving entitled "The Guards" depicts the church tower in the late nineteenth-century, prior to APVA preservation efforts.

"Tall trees grow in the churchyard which serve as haunt for blackbirds and crows, and add to the Gloom of the Prospect." The Ruins of Jamestown *by H. J. Brent, painted 1845, oil on canvas.*
APVA Preservation Virginia collection

Although new research has suggested that the church did not bear its distinctive tower until the last decade of the seventeenth century, this drawing of the church surrounded by parishioners made in the 1950s by Virginia artist Sidney King gives a sense of the church as the center of the Jamestown community.

The Relevance of the Church in Colonial Life

Maintaining a viable church in the new colony was important to the colonists for political, religious and social reasons. In the seventeenth century, membership in the Church of England was considered part of citizenship in the English nation. The idea of "separation of church and state" was inconceivable at the time.

The charter from King James I instructed the colonists to spread Christianity. It read:
> *Propagating of Christian religion to suche people as yet live in darkenesse and miserable ignorance of the true knoweledge and worshippe of God and may in tyme bring the infidels and salvages living in those parts to humane civilitie and to a setled and quiet govermente, doe by theise our lettres patents graciously accepte of and agree to theire humble and well intended desires.*

Later, the Virginia Assembly would reinforce this idea with legislation that required colonists to adhere to the canons of the Church of England "as neere as can be," given their conditions in a strange new land. "As neere as can be" meant that there were Sunday services, a weekday sermon and during the early years of the settlement, there were daily prayers. Holy Communion was celebrated on Christmas, Easter and Whitsunday and perhaps more often. A Reverend Whitaker wrote in 1614, that Virginia parishes celebrated Communion once a month and yearly offered a "solemn fast."

However, some adaptations were necessary in this new environment. Although spiritual motivation was important, so was the profit motive. Many settlers had come seeking gold and found it in the tobacco plant. Therefore, if two holy days fell consecutively during the growing season (March through September), only the first would be observed.

The interplay of light and shadow inside the old tower evokes an image of ages past.

Most people probably attended services willingly. However, if the church leaders at Jamestown adhered to the practices of the Church of England as mandated, absenteeism could result in stiff penalties, such as having to pay a fine or being excommunicated from the church. In fact, one of the laws passed by the first Virginia Assembly made church attendance compulsory.

There were graver consequences for other offenses against the church. Under the colonial legal code—the Lawes Divine, Morall and Martiall—colonists could be put to death for blasphemy or stealing from the church, and could be whipped for demeaning a preacher.

In the seventeenth century the church was the center of the secular as well as the religious community. It was a social outlet where neighbors could visit, share news and conduct business. The church was a communications center where important messages were posted or read from the pulpit. Like the parish churches in England, it could also have been used as a schoolhouse or storage area for grain or the militia's weapons. And of course the church was used for meetings of the General Assembly beginning in 1619.

The church reflected colonial government at

Olde Church Tower- 1639 — James Towne, Va —

A colorized postcard of the Tower and Memorial Church, circa 1915.
APVA Preservation Virginia collection

its most basic level. The parish vestry was composed of many of the same men who served on the House of Burgesses, on the county court and in other influential positions in the colony. They had the power to levy tithes and responsibility for caring for less fortunate parishioners.

The parish minister had a dual role within the community. He not only led his flock in worship according to the *Book of Common Prayer*, but served as a liaison between the government and the settlers. The Virginia Assembly charged parish ministers with seeking to prevent "all ungodly disorders."

Descriptions of the worship services at Jamestown offer additional insight into the religious as well as social customs of the times.

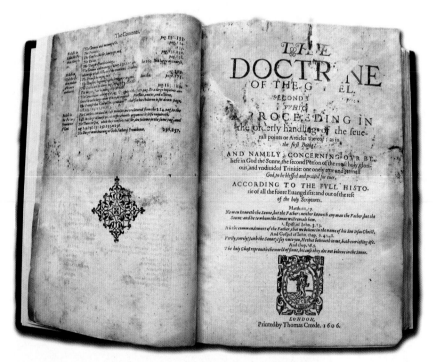

This religious text entitled Doctrine of the Gospel *and published in 1606—the same year the Jamestown settlers departed Virginia for England—is an example of the type of religious text that the religious leaders of the Jamestown colony would have been intimately familiar with.*
APVA Preservation Virginia collection

For instance, the status of each parishioner dictated where he or she would sit in the church.

The most prominent citizens, such as government officials or the vestry members, would sit in the front, near the chancel. William Strachey in 1610 described how the Governor of Virginia, Lord De La Warr "hath his seate in the Quier, in a greene Velvet Chair, with a Cloath, with a Velvet Cushion spread on a Table before him, on which he kneeleth, and on each side sit the Counsell, Captaines and Officers, each in their place." Those of lower social standing sat in the back of the church. Gender was also a factor, with men typically seated on the north side of the church and women on the south side.

The actual services in the Jamestown Church mirrored those in England, following the *Book of Common Prayer* and other ecclesiastical laws. There were morning and afternoon services on Sundays, as well as a weekday sermon. Strachey wrote in 1610 that there were daily prayer services, with the church bell ringing at 10:00 in the morning and at 4:00 in the afternoon, "when each man addresseth himselfe to prayers."

Anglican services, according to historian Keith Thomas, were designed to emphasize social solidarity and citizenship. Thus "common prayer" was a collective act which affirmed the common concerns of the parishioners. In the case of Jamestown, that meant preserving order and harmony crucial to the settlers' survival. In other words, common prayer was for the common good.

This engraving, entitled "Ruins at Jamestown" is from the 1846 edition of Henry Howe's book Historical Collections of Virginia *and shows that the church was in ruins by the middle of the nineteenth century. APVA Preservation Virginia collection*

The Jamestown Communion Silver

Certain physical objects were essential to the practice of the Anglican faith in the seventeenth century and each parish church would have owned a set. In 1610, William Strachey enumerated many of these in his description of the Jamestown Church in its early years: *"A Chancell in it of cedar, and a Communion Table of the Blake Walnut, and all the Pewes of cedar, with faire broad windowes, to shut and open, as the weather shall occasion, of the same wood, a Pulpet of the same, with a Font hewen hollow, like a Canoa, with two Bels at the West end. It is so cast, as it be very light within, and trimmed up with divers flowers, with a Sexton belonging to it."*

The first pieces used at Jamestown were fairly basic. However, as the church became more established, it acquired more and better pieces. Only a few of these ecclesiastical objects survive today. Those pieces that were lost may have been given away or melted down and the metal reused for other purposes. Some of the ecclesiastical objects of the Jamestown Church, specifically the communion silver and baptismal font, developed a very interesting history of their own.

A few of the surviving pieces are believed to have been given to Bruton Parish Church after the church at Jamestown was abandoned in the 1750s. Sue Godson, historian of Bruton Parish Church, notes that the Jamestown church service consisted of an oversized (10-¾ inches) chalice and a 7-inch paten (a plate usually made of precious metal and used to carry the bread at the Eucharist). The chalice and paten are believed to have been given to the Jamestown Church in 1661 by the deputy governor,

Silver chalice and paten, circa 1661. Both pieces of communion silver were originally used at the Jamestown Church and are inscribed "Mixe not holy thinges with profane." They were given to the Bruton Parish Church in the mid eighteenth century.
Photo courtesy Bruton Parish Church, Williamsburg, Virginia

Silver alms basin, circa 1739–40, inscribed "For the Use of James City County Parish Church." Courtesy Bruton Parish Church, Williamsburg, Virginia

Colonel Francis Morrison. Both are inscribed "Mixe not holy thinges with profane." The third piece of the communion silver is an alms basin, circa 1739–40, inscribed "For the Use of James City County Parish Church." In 1827, the Bruton Parish vestry lent the silver to the Reverend John Grammer to use in any churches under his care. He turned the set over to the Virginia Diocesan Convention in 1854, and that body deposited it in the library of the Virginia Theological Seminary. After the Bruton vestry requested its return, the three-piece set made it back to Williamsburg in 1859.

Along with the communion silver, the Jamestown baptismal font now resides at Bruton Parish Church. Described as an octagonal bowl carved of gray stone resting on an octagonal limestone pedestal, the font is located in the Governor's Pew. Like many of the Jamestown Church artifacts, it had a circuitous journey as well. After the Jamestown Church fell into disuse in the 1750s, the font was moved a couple of miles away to the new Church on the Main. After that church was abandoned, the font likely was taken to the Powder Magazine in Williamsburg. It finally ended up at Bruton Parish around 1758 and has been in use there ever since.

The baptismal font from the Jamestown Church is now located in the Governor's pew at Bruton Parish Church. Photo courtesy Bruton Parish Church, Williamsburg, Virginia

"The ultimate goal of every preservation effort is to resist time as gently as we can."

—Louis Malon, Director of Preservation Services, APVA Preservation Virginia

Chapter Two
Preservervation and the APVA

Study drawing for the restoration of the Jamestown church, completed by Samuel H. Yonge for his book The Site of Old "James Towne" 1607–1698.
APVA Preservation Virginia collection

On January 4, 1889, a development took place that would have far-reaching impact on the Jamestown Church. Mary Jeffery Galt of Norfolk and Cynthia Beverley Tucker Coleman of Williamsburg founded the Association for the Preservation of Virginia Antiquities (now APVA Preservation Virginia). The new organization's mission was clear: "to restore and preserve the ancient historic buildings and tombs in the State of Virginia, and acquire by purchase or gift the sites of such buildings and tombs with a view to their perpetuation and preservation."

"These stubborn ladies doing good," as the early members of the APVA were once described, were part of the vanguard of the preservation movement that saved the Jamestown Church and many important landmarks from the "vortex of oblivion." Their other projects included the Mary Washington House in Fredericksburg, the Powder Magazine at Williamsburg, the John Marshall House in Richmond, and the Old Cape Henry Lighthouse in Virginia Beach.

Mary Jeffery Galt

Miss Mary Jeffery Galt of Norfolk was one of the driving forces behind the founding of the Association for the Preservation of Virginia Antiquities in 1889. Miss Galt was inspired by her mother, who was deeply concerned that "all our Virginia landmarks are passing away; nothing is being done to save them, before long all will be gone."

Miss Galt and the early founders of the APVA personified the "white gloves and red bricks" approach to preservation. These well-to-do ladies did not hesitate to get their hands dirty, literally or figuratively, doing excavation work, pulling weeds or buttonholing legislators, all for the benefit of saving important Virginia historical relics.

Miss Galt served as APVA Vice President from 1889 until 1898 and then as Honorary Vice President until her death in 1922. During her tenure with the APVA she led many of the early preservation and archaeological activities at the site of the Jamestown church tower.

Miss Mary Jeffery Galt, one of the founders of the Association for the Preservation of Virginia Antiquities.

Although they occupied themselves for several years with saving threatened historic sites across the Commonwealth, from the beginning the ladies of the APVA set their sights on acquiring the Jamestown church tower and surrounding land. They worried that the James River was encroaching on the site of the 1607 fort and felt immediate action was needed to save this nationally important site from permanent destruction.

Ownership of the site of the abandoned church tower and graveyard had reverted to the Colony of Virginia, and later the Commonwealth of Virginia, when the church fell out of use in the 1750s. The APVA leaders went to the General Assembly beginning in January 1890 to negotiate with the Commonwealth to deed the property to them as permanent stewards for its preservation. On April 19, 1892 it was recorded that the General Assembly had passed an act giving the APVA the right to have and hold the church ruins and graveyard at Jamestown.

Next the APVA's leaders began court proceedings seeking right-of-way access to the Church. This action was ended in January 1893 when the new owners of the land on Jamestown Island, Mr. and Mrs. Edward Barney, gave 22.5 acres of land surrounding the church tower to the APVA. The Barneys had purchased the land at Jamestown in late 1892. Mr. Barney did not agree that the Commonwealth had the right to give the church ruins to the APVA. However, he was personally interested in the Association and wanted to turn the property over to the APVA himself. With the encouragement of Mrs. Barney, he deeded the acreage to the Association. The Barneys' gift made it possible for the APVA to have sufficient ingress and egress to the church property and helped set in motion their monumental task of preserving the historic church site. It also earned Mr. Barney a lifetime membership in the APVA.

After the Virginia General Assembly conveyed the church tower and graveyard to the APVA in 1892, the Association's first goal was to protect the property from the erosion which had damaged the shoreline. Mary Jeffery Galt was placed in charge of the property and she quickly got to work coordinating efforts to preserve the site.

In 1894, Congress appropriated $10,000 for the United States Army Corps of Engineers to construct a temporary breakwater of granite. It would protect the shoreline from erosion that was threatening the site where the remains of early settlements were thought to have been located.

The construction of the breakwater led to a dispute between the APVA and

The Barney Monument

In addition to their gift of land to the APVA, the Barneys initiated many improvements to Jamestown Island to make it more accessible to visitors. They built a wooden wharf that extended 200 feet into the James River where steamers bearing tourists could dock. They reclaimed acres of marsh land and cultivated crops. They built a new bridge and improved the road across the marsh. The monument to Mr. and Mrs. Barney was erected by the APVA in appreciation of their donation of land and support of the preservation efforts. It reads:

IN LASTING GRATITUDE TO
MR. AND MRS. EDWARD E. BARNEY
FOR THE GIFT OF THIS HISTORIC GROUND
MAY 3, 1893

PLACED BY THE ASSOCIATION
FOR THE PRESERVATION OF
VIRGINIA ANTIQUITIES
1912

the federal government. According to APVA officials, government contractors committed "depredations" to the property, digging up relics and damaging the grounds. Miss Galt said that the army's "twenty-seven mules and heavy machinery undid much of what we had done to improve the place. After they left, we remade the road, planted more trees, sowed grass, planted flowers and had some filling in and evening up of the grounds done."

In 1896 Congress allocated another $15,000 for the construction of a permanent seawall to replace the temporary breakwater. But because of the dispute, construction of the seawall was delayed until about the turn of the century. Mr. Samuel H. Yonge with the

The construction of the seawall around 1900 was an important step in halting the erosion of the Jamestown shoreline.

United States Army Corps of Engineers oversaw this important effort. These efforts to preserve the shoreline saved the remains of the 1607 fort which was found during the Jamestown Rediscovery® excavations in the 1990s.

Preservation of the church ruins began in 1896. The APVA hired architect Howard Constable. He strengthened the tower with iron rods, had the bushes and vines growing in the top bricks removed and cemented the top of the tower so it would shed rain.

In 1897, Miss Galt and Miss Mary W. Garrett began the initial excavations of the church ruins. Miss Galt reported, "I dug with my own hands… and discovered the little inner wall composed of large bricks and cobblestones." This marked the amazing discovery of two separate foundations. The cobblestone inner foundation would have been too light to support a brick structure. They

During the excavation of the early 1900s, the workers unearthed the grave of one of the early ministers, John Clough.

The ladies of the APVA conducted excavations in the late 1890s and early 1900s which led to the surprising discovery of two separate foundations.

reached the conclusion that this was the foundation of the 1617 frame church. The outer foundation of brick must have supported the brick church that was built in the 1640s or 1650s.

More formal excavations began in 1901. John Tyler, a federal engineer, and William Leal, a local stonemason, assisted the ladies. They discovered evidence of a fire in the chancel and three distinct tile floors at different levels, indicating that there were three churches on the same site. One of the high points of their excavation was the discovery of the knight's tomb, which at the time was believed to be that of Sir George Yeardley, who was Governor of the colony in 1619 when the first Assembly convened. The team also unearthed the grave of one of the early ministers, John Clough.

In 1901, during the excavations led by Miss Galt, numerous graves were discovered in and around the church. Work notes relate that, "One grave we opened contained the skeleton of a woman—on her breast the scant remains of a tiny little skeleton—the little head by her cheek—and two little skeletons, evidently previous interment, just under her feet."

A photo of the church tower prior to the preservation efforts of the late 1890s.

Myths and Legends of The Jamestown Church: The Knight's Tomb

The Knight's Tomb, located at the east end of the Jamestown Church, has long been believed to mark the grave of Sir George Yeardley. Yeardley served several times as Governor of Virginia and was knighted by King James I in 1618. As Governor, he called the first representative legislative assembly to meet in the church at Jamestown. Yeardley died at Jamestown in 1627. This gravestone originally carried monumental brasses, consisting of brass depictions of a helmeted knight in armor with an inscription plate, a shield and scroll, and a border all set into the stone tomb. The depressions in the stone indicate where the insets would have been; however the brasses were removed prior to the acquisition of the church by the APVA and their current location is unknown. The brass made this tombstone unique for an American colonial site.

Today historians are less certain that this tomb belonged to Yeardley. Instead it may house the remains of Lord De La Warr or another prominent early resident of Jamestown.

Miss Galt and her team studied the contents of about 50 graves. The excavations that took place in 1906 were of particular importance. This is when the crew dug across the chancel of the church where they found ten graves. They discovered bones, nails and bits of clay pipe. They also became convinced that the Knight's Tomb, discovered in 1901, was indeed that of Governor Sir George Yeardley based on the assumption that, in accordance with European tradition, only royalty and nobility would have been buried inside the church. With the 300th anniversary of the founding of Jamestown approaching in 1907, such news generated great excitement.

Work on the church ruins and the island proceeded steadily in preparation for the 300th anniversary of Jamestown in 1907. There was a strong feeling throughout the Commonwealth that Virginians should not allow New Englanders to continue to "steal the thunder" by promoting Plymouth as the birthplace of America.

Years before the anniversary arrived, APVA officials had conveyed to other heritage organizations the need to make a splash at Jamestown. Accordingly, the National Society of The Colonial Dames of America voted to donate $6,000 to build a permanent memorial building at Jamestown. This would become the Memorial Church that stands beside the old tower today.

The Memorial Church was modeled on the St. Luke's Church or "Old Brick Church" near Smithfield, believed to be the oldest surviving Protestant church in America. At the time the church was thought to date to about 1632, although recent scholarship suggests that it may perhaps have been built later, around 1682. The Jamestown Memorial Church has buttressed walls similar to those of St. Luke's. Other architectural elements in common are a tower at the west end of each church and a chancel door on the south side. The brickwork of St. Luke's is different, however. It is laid in the more decorative style of Flemish bond, whereas the brickwork of the Jamestown Church is English bond.

The efforts of the APVA to preserve the Jamestown Church culminated with the construction of the Memorial Church adjacent to the old tower. A sister organization, the Society of Colonial Dames of America, presented the building, which cost $6,000, to the APVA in 1907.

The Jamestown Memorial Church was modeled after St. Luke's Church in Smithfield. Prominent Boston architects Edmund Wheelwright and Ralph Adams Cram designed the Jamestown Church.

This view of St. Luke's shows how similar the two churches are in design. St. Luke's is said to be the oldest surviving Protestant church in America.

The tower of the Jamestown Church.

The tower of St. Luke's.

These two views show the similarity of the brickwork of the two churches. At left is the Jamestown Church. At right is St. Luke's.

Details of the English bond brickwork at the Jamestown Church (left) and the Flemish bond at St. Luke's Church (right).

The Jamestown Memorial Church was constructed over the foundations that had been uncovered by the APVA archaeologists and adjacent, but not connected to the old tower ruins. When no manufacturer could be found to replicate the brick in the surviving tower, the National Society of the Colonial Dames of America purchased two buildings considered "colonial ruins" in Hampton, Virginia and salvaged those old bricks for use in the Memorial Church. This was a technique considered appropriate at the time but is not used by preservationists today.

The foundations of the 1617 church are carefully preserved under glass.

On May 11, 1907, the Jamestown Memorial Church was presented by the National Society of the Colonial Dames of America to the APVA. The church was a focal point of the Tercentennial, or 300th anniversary, celebrations at Jamestown. A year later, on May 13, 1908, the Memorial Church was formally dedicated. Mrs. Kate Cabell Cox, chairman of the services of dedication, wrote: "Thus the little memorial building erected to preserve precious fragments of the past was dedicated by prayer, praise and words of wisdom and will forevermore be the joint possession of all Christian people for the service of the Almighty."

Throughout the twentieth century and into the twenty-first, the APVA has worked steadfastly to protect, study, and interpret the Jamestown Church to the public. Ongoing preservation work such as repointing bricks and repairing mortar using appropriate local replacement materials has helped to ensure that the seventeenth-century tower and the now 100-year-old Jamestown Memorial Church will survive for future generations of Virginians to enjoy.

The Chancel ends of the Jamestown Memorial Church (above) and St. Lukes Church (below).

Since it was built in 1907, millions of visitors have toured the church. Although never consecrated, the Jamestown Memorial Church has been the site of a variety of commemorative services over the past 100 years and today can be rented for weddings and other special events.

New research continues to reshape how historians view the Jamestown Church. The church tower, long thought to have been built in the 1630s, is now believed to have been added much later, in the 1690s. Although the site of the first church has not yet been located, the search continues and the archaeological discoveries of the Jamestown Rediscovery® project have helped to shed new light on the lives of the men and women who built and worshiped at the church.

Services in the Old Church

Postcard circa 1947 showing the Rev. W. A. R. Goodwin conducting services commemorating the arrival of the settlers in 1607. Goodwin was closely involved in the restoration at nearby Colonial Williamsburg.

Miss Ellen Bagby

She was called the "Queen of Jamestown" for her 30 years of service to the Jamestown Festival Committee and the APVA. Known for her wit, Miss Ellen Bagby (or Miss Ellen, as she was often called) sometimes offered herself as proof of the APVA's success, saying, "If there was a Virginia antiquity well-preserved, it's me."

Ellen Bagby was born in Richmond in 1879, the daughter of Dr. George W. Bagby, author of *The Old Virginia Gentleman and Other Sketches.* Her mother, Mrs. Lucy Parke Chamberlayne Bagby, was active in the APVA and Miss Ellen's own involvement began at the age of 17 when she was a May pole dancer at an APVA function in 1896.

From 1930 to 1960, Miss Bagby worked tirelessly to promote and protect Jamestown. She considered it a sacred shrine and expected all visitors to share her enthusiasm. She considered a visit to Jamestown to be the most important historic experience of a lifetime. In her position as chairman of the Jamestown Committee of the APVA, she welcomed many prominent visitors to Jamestown, including film maker Cecil B. DeMille in 1940 and Vice President Richard M. Nixon in 1957. Nixon drew her ire when he kept referring to the importance of the Mayflower, which brought the Pilgrims to Plymouth Rock. This was a grievous error to make in the company of those who have worked mightily to correct the history books in favor of Jamestown as the true birthplace of America.

In 1960, Miss Ellen was presented with a special medal that had been struck in her honor by Bill deMatteo, the silversmith of Williamsburg. Mr. Carlisle Hummelsine of Colonial Williamsburg presented the medal to her and described her as follows: "As much as the seawall, or the ancient church tower, the stones of the churchyard, or the bared foundations of the early seventeenth century, Miss Ellen has come to mean Jamestown to modern Virginians. As Virginians and Americans we are in debt to her... She has been a kind of historical archangel."

APVA Preservation Virginia collection

Miss Ellen Bagby (far right) at Jamestown in 1935.

36

Sam Robinson

Sam Robinson, a native of Canada, was the caretaker and guide at the Jamestown Church during the tourist seasons from 1936 until his death in 1965. During the winter months he worked for Miss Bagby as a domestic employee in Richmond.

Ellen Bagby thought of Robinson as a Jamestown attraction in his own right, due to his entertaining way with visitors. His colorful, though fictional story of the so-called Mother-in-Law tree endeared him to visitors to Jamestown, (including Queen Elizabeth II) if not to historians. He was so well known that an issue of *Reader's Digest* in the 1950s had a picture of Sam on the back cover talking to tourists.

In the summer of 1964 Robinson became ill and he died the next year in Richmond where he is buried.

Old sycamore tree, Jamestown, Va., separating the tombs of the Rev. James Blair and his wife. Sam Robinson, the guide, in attendance.

Postcard depicting Sam Robinson standing in front of The Mother-in-Law Tree.
APVA Preservation Virginia collection

Myths and Legends of The Jamestown Church: The Mother-in-Law Tree

Sam Robinson's trademark speech perpetuated the myth surrounding the tombstones of the Reverend James Blair and his wife Sarah Harrison Blair in the graveyard. Reverend Blair was the Anglican commissary of Virginia in the 1690s and the founder of the College of William and Mary. A sycamore tree grew up between his tomb and that of his wife. The story goes that this happened because her parents had opposed their marriage, thinking Blair was too old. The sycamore came to be known as the Mother-in-Law Tree. Queen Elizabeth's request to hear the story was sparked by the fact that the Queen Mother heard the tale of the Mother-in-Law Tree from Robinson during her visit to Jamestown in 1954.

To The Glory Of God
And In Grateful Remembrance Of
The Adventurers In England
And
Ancient Planters In Virginia
Who Through Evil Report
And Loss Of Fortune
Through Suffering And Death
Maintained Stout Hearts
And Laid The Foundations
Of Our Country

This Building Is Erected By The
National Society Of Colonial Dames
Of America
To Commemorate The
Three Hundredth Anniversary Of
The Landing Of The
First Permanent English Settlers
Upon American Soil
1607 The 13th Of May 1907

–From the dedication plaque inside the
Jamestown Memorial Church,
National Society of Colonial Dames, 1907

Chapter Three
The Jamestown Church Today

The 1907 Memorial Church
By Louis Malon, Director of Preservation Services, APVA Preservation Virginia

As the nation and the APVA prepared to commemorate the 300th anniversary of the founding of the first permanent English settlement in 1907, the National Society of the Colonial Dames of America determined to make their contribution by recreating the church building that once stood along with the tower at Jamestown. As both organizations were composed of volunteers, the Colonial Dames sought advice and guidance from prominent Boston architects such as Edmund Wheelwright and Ralph Adams Cram.

The Colonial Dames and their advisors chose St. Luke's Church in nearby Smithfield as a guide. St. Luke's is the oldest existing church of English foundation in America and the nation's only surviving Gothic building. Cram, the pre-eminent designer of churches and academic buildings in the Gothic style, was among the most renowned American architects of the twentieth century and the country's premier architectural designer of Gothic and ecclesiastical buildings. To provide authentic materials for the construction, the Colonial Dames secured early bricks from period buildings that were being demolished. The perfect gathering of model, designer and materials yielded a structure so well suited to its site and setting as to give rise to the misleading impression that it too is a seventeenth-century building.

The building that still stands today matches the dimensions of the 1617 church and sits just outside its foundations. The integrity of those foundations is not compromised and they are revealed under glass-covered trenches that run the length of the church walls. The floor of the nave has been kept low to match the remaining foundation layer. The chancel is elevated by an introduced wooden floor that too is pierced to display early tiles and grave markings found in place.

Four sets of robust buttresses support the walls and form the north enclosing wall, which approached, but does not touch the existing tower. The south end wall features an elaborate array of brick traceried windows forming a large arch. Each bay defined by the buttresses features double arched windows, again with moulded brick traceries. Both end walls have stepped gables (often referred to as either corbelled or crow-stepped gables), which reinforce the Gothic style. The roof is of slate.

The Memorial Church of 1907 is carefully joined to the brick tower, which serves as the entrance to the church. This tower was long thought to be the remains of the 1639-1649 church. Recent scholarship has shown it more likely to have been built following the destruction that occurred during Bacon's Rebellion of 1676. The most telling argument for this revised dating is the prominent compass headed arches over the main entry and the second floor window. According to architectural historians who have studied the structure extensively, the use of compass headed windows was rare in England until the massive rebuilding after the Great Fire of 1666 in London and did not enter Virginia building practice until the last quarter of the seventeenth-century. The church tower is now believed to be the only surviving element from the fifth church built at Jamestown. It remains as the only above ground structure that dates to the seventeenth-century at Historic Jamestowne.

The following exterior views of the Jamestown Church show the key architectural features of the building that are visible as one walks around the church.

The view from aboard the Jamestown Ferry.

The west elevation showing church and palisades.

A view of the south elevation, which faces the James River.

A southeastern perspective showing the graveyard and the brick wall surrounding it.

The eastern elevation, showing the graveyard and the James River.

A view of the church from its northern side with a partial brick wall and statue of Captain John Smith visible in the background.

A northwestern view of the church completes the circle.

Inside The Church

Visitors to the Jamestown Church may feel as though they have passed through a time portal when they walk through the dignified ruins of the old tower and enter the sanctuary of the Memorial Church. Inside they will see the original cobblestone foundations from the frame church of 1617 and the brick foundations from the first brick church. The Knight's Tomb is visible at the front of the church. Along the walls are 20 commemorative plaques.

This coat of arms, depicting the Stuart crest, was presented to the APVA in 1957 by Queen Elizabeth II. It features both the motto of the British monarchs—Dieu et mon droit (translated as "God and my right")—and the motto of the Order of the Garter—Honi soit qui mal y pense (which has been translated as "Evil to him who evil thinks" and "Shame on him who thinks ill of it") on a representation of the garter behind the shield.

The walls of the seventeenth-century tower frame the doorway of the Jamestown Memorial Church.

A closer view of the pews and chancel. Two black tablets with the Ten Commandments flank the windows.

The side of the church with plaques dedicated to Pocahontas and Captain John Smith.

The view from the altar.

The plaques on the walls of the church commemorate individuals or events important to the early history of Jamestown and Virginia. They were contributed by a variety of local and national groups and individuals beginning in 1907 and continuing through the 1960s. Out of concerns for the preservation of the building, new plaques are no longer added to the walls. The existing plaques vary considerably in style, material and lettering. What follows is a complete transcription of the text on each of the plaques from the church walls.

Moving clockwise after entering through the church tower, the plaques read as follows:

A slate plaque commemorating the dedication of the Memorial Church in 1907:

To The Glory Of God
And In Grateful Remembrance Of
The Adventurers In England
And
Ancient Planters In Virginia
Who Through Evil Report
And Loss Of Fortune
Through Suffering And Death
Maintained Stout Hearts
And Laid The Foundations
Of Our Country

This Building Is Erected By The
National Society Of Colonial Dames
Of America
To Commemorate The
Three Hundredth Anniversary Of
The Landing Of The
First Permanent English Settlers
Upon American Soil
1607 The 13th Of May 1907

A bronze plaque with raised letters:

JOHN ROLFE—AN ENGLISH GENTLEMAN
CAME TO VIRGINIA IN 1610 AND DIED IN 1622
HE WAS A MEMBER OF COUNCIL
AND SECRETARY OF STATE
IN 1614 HIS MARRIAGE WITH POCAHONTAS CAUSED A PERIOD OF GOOD
FEELING BETWEEN THE INDIANS AND THE COLONISTS.
AS A MEMBER OF THE GENERAL ASSEMBLY OF VIRGINIA IN 1619
HE WAS ONE OF THE FOUNDERS OF AMERICAN DEMOCRACY.
HIS INTRODUCTION OF THE CULTIVATION OF TOBACCO IN 1612
AND HIS MAKING THE FIRST SHIPMENT OF TOBACCO FROM VIRGINIA
TO ENGLAND, MADE HIM THE PIONEER OF A GREAT INDUSTRY WHICH HAS
PROFOUNDLY AFFECTED THE ECONOMIC, SOCIAL AND BUSINESS
HISTORY OF OUR COUNTRY.

-.-

THE TOBACCO ASSOCIATION OF THE UNITED
STATES HAS ERECTED THIS MEMORIAL
AS A GRATEFUL TRIBUTE TO HIS MEMORY
A. D. 1926

IN GRATEFUL MEMORY
OF
THOMAS WEST
THIRD BARON DELAWARE
GOVERNOR OF VIRGINIA
1609
SAVIOUR OF THE COLONY
IN THE STARVING TIME OF
1610
HE DIED ON HIS SECOND
VOYAGE TO VIRGINIA
1618

This white stone plaque was given by Mrs. De Benneville Keim in 1907. Lord De La Warr (also spelled Delaware as on this plaque) was considered by many to be the savior of the colony because his ship arrived with much needed provisions during the spring of 1610 following the starving time.

IN MEMORY OF
CHANCO
AN INDIAN YOUTH CONVERTED TO
CHRISTIANITY WHO RESIDED IN THE
HOUSEHOLD OF RICHARD PACE
ACROSS THE RIVER FROM JAMESTOWN AND
WHO, ON THE EVE OF THE INDIAN MASSACRE
OF MARCH 22, 1622, WARNED PACE OF THE
MURDEROUS PLOT, THUS ENABLING PACE
TO CROSS THE RIVER IN A CANOE
TO ALERT AND SAVE THE JAMESTOWN
SETTLEMENT FROM IMPENDING DISASTER

ERECTED BY THE SOCIETY OF COLONIAL
DAMES OF AMERICA IN THE STATE OF VIRGINIA

This plaque in honor of the Indian youth Chanco was given by the Society of Colonial Dames of America in the State of Virginia in 1908.

TO THE GLORY OF GOD
AND TO THE HONORED MEMORY OF
WILLIAM CLAIBORNE
SON OF THOMAS CLEYBORNE OF
CRAYFORD, KENT GENTLEMAN, AND
SARA SMITH—JAMES. BORN 1587
SETTLED IN VIRGINIA 1621 MEMBER OF
COUNCIL 1625–60 TREASURER 1642–50
DEPUTY GOVERNOR 1653 COMMANDED
EXPEDITIONS AGAINST THE INDIANS 1629
& 1644 AT KENT ISLAND HE MADE THE
FIRST SETTLEMENT WITHIN THE
PRESENT BOUNDARY OF MARYLAND

The plaque in honor of William Claiborne was given by Mrs. W. R. Cox and Mrs. S. B. Buckner in 1907. Claiborne served as deputy governor of Virginia in 1653 among other offices. His birth date has since been found to be 1600, not 1587 as noted on the plaque.

IN MEMORY OF
JOHN POTT, M.A.
LEARNED DOCTOR
OF MEDICINE
PHYSICIAN GENERAL
MEMBER OF THE COUNCIL
GOVERNOR OF THE COLONY
Resident of Jamestown
1621 ~ 1635
ERECTED IN 1950 BY THE MEDICAL SOCIETY OF VIRGINIA

A white marble plaque was given by the Medical Society of Virginia in 1950. Pott was the first doctor in the colony.

CAPTAIN EDWARD MARIA WINGFIELD

Born about 1560, Son of Thomas Maria Wingfield, M.P., of Huntingdonshire, and Grandson of Sir Richard Wingfield, K.G., of Kimbolton Castle. A Valiant Soldier in the Armies of Queen Elizabeth in Ireland and in the Netherlands. But his Name is forever identified with this Hallowed Place, Jamestown, a Site which he selected, where English Civilization was First Established on American Soil. A Leading Factor in forming the Virginia Company of London. The Only Grantee in the Virginia Charter of 1606 who accompanied the First Settlers to these Shores. First President of the Council of Virginia. Despite Administrative Vexations encountered in 1607, his Faith in the Colonial Venture remained undimmed. Author in 1608 of "A Discourse of Virginia." A Grantee of the Colony in the Second Virginia Charter of 1609. A Generous Subscriber to the Subsequent Undertakings of the Virginia Company of London. Died at Stonely Priory, Huntingdonshire, England, after 1613.

The inscription on this white marble plaque dedicated to Captain Edward Maria Wingfield reads:

Born about 1560, Son of Thomas Maria Wingfield, M.P., of Huntingdonshire, K. G., of Kimbolton Castle. A Valiant Soldier in the Armies of Queen Elizabeth in Ireland and in the Netherlands. But his Name is forever identified with this Hallowed Place, Jamestown, a Site which he selected, where English Civilization was First established on American Soil. A Leading Factor in forming the Virginia Company of London. The Only Grantee in the Virginia Charter of 1606 who accompanied the First Settlers to these Shores. First President of the Council of Virginia. Despite Administrative Vexations encountered in 1607, his faith in the Colonial Venture remained undimmed. Author in 1608 of "A Discourse of Virginia." A Grantee of the Colony in the Second Virginia Charter of 1609. A Generous Subscriber to the Subsequent Undertakings of the Virginia Company of London. Died at Stonely Priory, Huntingdonshire, England, after 1613.

A bronze plaque in honor of Thomas Savage was erected by his descendants in 1931. It reads:

THOMAS SAVAGE, GENTLEMAN AND ENSIGN
THE FIRST WHITE SETTLER ON THE EASTERN SHORE OF VIRGINIA,
HOSTAGE TO POWHATAN, 1608, HIS LOYALTY AND
FEARLESSNESS ENDEARED HIM TO THE GREAT KING WHO TREATED HIM AS
HIS SON, WHILE HE RENDERED INVALUABLE AID TO THE COLONY AS INTERPRETER.
GREATLY BELOVED BY DEBEDEAVON, THE LAUGHING KING OF THE ACCAWMACKES.
HE WAS GIVEN A TRACT OF NINE THOUSAND ACRES OF LAND
KNOWN AS SAVAGE'S NECK.
HE OBTAINED FOOD FOR THE STARVING COLONY AT JAMESTOWN THROUGH HIS
FRIENDSHIP WITH THE KINDLY EASTERN SHORE INDIANS.
A RELATION OF HIS VOYAGES ON THE GREAT BAY IN SEARCH OF TRADE FOR THE
ENGLISH, WA READ BEFORE THE LONDON COMPANY AT A COURT HELD JULY 10TH, 1621.
JOHN PORY, SECRETARY OF THE COLONY SAYS: "HE WITH MUCH HONESTIE
AND GOOD SUCCESSE, SERVED THE PUBLIQUE WITHOUT ANY PUBLIQUE RECOMPENSE,
YET HAD AN ARROW SHOT THROUGH HIS BODY IN THEIR SERVICE.

"YOU BRAVE HEROIC MINDS,
WORTHY YOUR COUNTRY'S NAME
THAT HONOR STILL PURSUE,
GO AND SUBDUE
WHILST LOITERING HINDS
LURK HERE AT HOME, WITH SHAME."

ERECTED BY SOME OF HIS DESCENDANTS
1931

This bronze plaque honoring George Sandys was written in Latin.

GEORGIO SANDYS · PRIMO POETAE AMERICANO
QVI DVM QVAESTOR AERARII COLONIAE VIRGINIAE ERAT
OVIDI METAMORPHOSES
IN VERSVS ANGLICOS TRANSTVLIT
ITAQVE IN NOSTRIS ORIS OPVS CLASSICVM PRIMVM EDIDIT
QVI AVTEM IN TERRIS NOVIS NEMPE
INTER OMNIA SILVESTRIA
QVAMVIS IPSE FINITIMIS CIRCVMSONARETVR ARMIS
SEMINA TAMEN RERVM HVMANIORVM SEVIT
QVAS NOS POSTERI PER
VASTVM CONTINENTEM FLORENTES VIDIMVS
IDCIRCO EI HOC MONVMENTVM
HONORIS CAVSA · D.D.D.
ERECTED BY THE FRIENDS OF THE CLASSICS IN AMERICA
UNDER THE AUSPICES OF THE CLASSICAL ASSOCIATION OF VIRGINIA
1929

Translated: To George Sandys, The First American Poet, Who While He Was Treasurer Of The Colony Of Virginia Translated Ovid's Metamorphoses Into English Verse And Thus Produced The First Classical Word On Our Soil, And Who Also, In Spite Of Being In A New Country Where All Was Wilderness And He Himself Was Surrounded By The Clash Of Neighboring Arms, Nevertheless Sowed The Seeds Of The Humanities Which We Now See Flourishing Throughout A Vast Continent. Therefore In His Honor This Monument Is Dedicated.

In English: Erected By The Friends Of The Classics In America. Under The Auspices Of The Classical Association Of Virginia
1929

The Ten Commaundements

i.
Thou shalt haue none other gods but me.

ii.
Thou shalt not make to thy selfe any grauen image.

iii.
Thou shalt not take the Name of the Lord thy God in Vaine.

iiii.
Remember that thou keepe holy the Sabboth day.

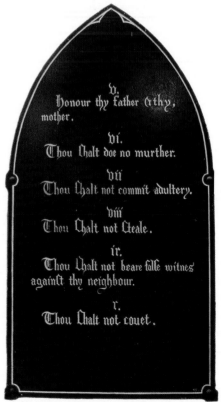

v.
Honour thy father & thy mother.

vi.
Thou shalt doe no murther.

vii
Thou shalt not commit adultery.

viii
Thou shalt not steale.

ix.
Thou shalt not beare false witnes against thy neighbour.

x.
Thou shalt not couet.

Wooden tablets with the Ten Cammandments are mounted above the altar. Presented by the Jamestown Chapter of the National Society Colonial Daughters of the Seventeenth Century in 1957.

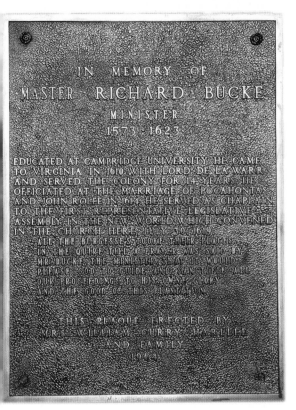

Bronze plaque memorializing Minister Richard Bucke reads as follows:

IN MEMORY OF
MASTER RICHARD BUCKE
MINISTER
1573–1623
EDUCATED AT CAMBRIDGE UNIVERSITY, HE CAME
TO VIRGINIA IN 1610 WITH LORD DE LA WARR
AND SERVED THE COLONY FOR 14 YEARS. HE
OFFICIATED AT THE MARRIAGE OF POCAHONTAS
AND JOHN ROLFE IN 1614. HE SERVED AS CHAPLAIN
TO THE FIRST REPRESENTATIVE LEGISLATIVE
ASSEMBLY IN THE NEW WORLD WHICH CONVENED
IN THE CHURCH HERE, JULY 30, 1619.
ALL THE BURGESSE'S TOOKE THEIR PLACES
IN THE QUIRE TILL A PRAYER WAS SAID BY
MR. BUCKE, THE MINISTER, THAT IT WOULD
PLEASE GOD TO GUIDE AND SANCTIFIE ALL
OUR PROCEEDINGS TO HIS OWNE GLORY
AND THE GOOD OF THIS PLANTATION.

THIS PLAQUE ERECTED BY
MRS. WILLIAM CURRY HARLLEE
AND FAMILY
1964

This plaque in honor of Major Daniel Gookin was donated by the Massachusetts Society of the Colonial Dames of America.

IN MEMORY OF
MAJOR GENERAL DANIEL GOOKIN
AºD! 1612 – 1687
A PLANTER OF VIRGINIA AND LATER A PILLAR
OF THE COLONY OF MASSACHUSETTS BAY
A SOLDIER A STATESMAN AND ABOVE ALL
A CONSTANT FRIEND AND GUARDIAN
OF THE NATIVE INDIANS OF NEW ENGLAND

This tablet is placed here by the
Massachusetts Society of the
Colonial Dames of America

THE COMMON LAW

HERE THE COMMON LAW OF ENGLAND WAS ESTABLISHED ON THIS CONTINENT WITH THE ARRIVAL OF THE FIRST SETTLERS ON MAY 13,1607. THE FIRST CHARTER GRANTED BY JAMES I TO THE VIRGINIA COMPANY IN 1606 DECLARED THAT THE INHABITANTS OF THE COLONY"...SHALL HAVE AND ENJOY ALL LIBERTIES, FRANCHISES AND IMMUNITIES... AS IF THEY HAD BEEN ABIDING AND BORNE WITHIN THIS OUR REALME OF ENGLANDE...". SINCE MAGNA CARTA THE COMMON LAW HAS BEEN THE CORNERSTONE OF INDIVIDUAL LIBERTIES, EVEN AS AGAINST THE CROWN. SUMMARIZED LATER IN THE BILL OF RIGHTS ITS PRINCIPLES HAVE INSPIRED THE DEVELOPMENT OF OUR SYSTEM OF FREEDOM UNDER LAW, WHICH IS AT ONCE OUR DEAREST POSSESSION AND PROUDEST ACHIEVEMENT.

PRESENTED BY THE VIRGINIA STATE BAR MAY 17, 1959

A marble plaque honors Jamestown as the site where Common Law was first established in America. It was placed by the Virginia State Bar in 1959.

A plaque honoring Captain John Smith and bearing his coat of arms was given by the Washington Branch of the APVA in 1907. It is a replica of the tablet at St. Sepulchre's Church, London, England where Smith is buried.

To the living memory of his deceased friend
Captaine John Smith
sometime Governor of Virginia
and Admirall of New England
who departed this life the 21st of June 1631.
"Accordamus vincere est vivere."
Here lies one conquer'd who hath conquer'd Kings
Subdu'd large Territories and done things
Which to the World impossible would seeme
But that the Truth is held in more esteeme
Shall I report his former service done
In honour of his God and Christendome:
How that he did divide from Pagans three
Their Heads and Lives, Types of his Chivalry
For which great service in that climate done
Brave Sigismundus (King of Hungarion,)
Did give him as a Coat of Armes to weare
Those conquer'd heads got by his Sword and Speare
Or shall I tell of his Adventures since,
Done in Virginia, that large Continence?
How that he subdu'd Kings unto his Yoke
And made those heathen flie as wind doth smoke
And made their land, being of so large a Station,
A Habitation for our Christian Nation
Where God is glorifi'd, their wants suppli'd
Which else for Necessaries, Must have dy'd
Butt what availes his Conquests now he lyes
Interr'd in Earth a Prey for Wormes and Flies?
O may his Soule in sweet Elysium sleepe
Until the Keeper that all Soules dothe Keepe
Returne to Judgment, and that after thence
With Angels he may have his Recompense.

Replica of Tablet St. Sepulchre's Church, London, Eng. Presented by the Washington Branch A.P.V.A. May, 1907

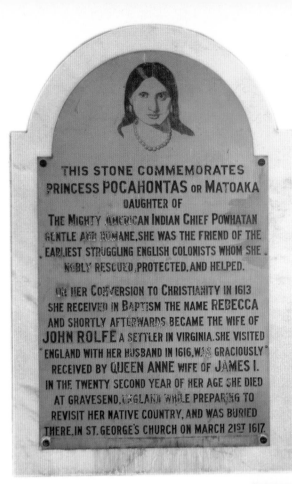

THIS STONE COMMEMORATES
PRINCESS POCAHONTAS OR MATOAKA
DAUGHTER OF
THE MIGHTY AMERICAN INDIAN CHIEF POWHATAN
GENTLE AND HUMANE, SHE WAS THE FRIEND OF THE
EARLIEST STRUGGLING ENGLISH COLONISTS WHOM SHE
NOBLY RESCUED, PROTECTED, AND HELPED.

ON HER CONVERSION TO CHRISTIANITY IN 1613
SHE RECEIVED IN BAPTISM THE NAME REBECCA
AND SHORTLY AFTERWARDS BECAME THE WIFE OF
JOHN ROLFE A SETTLER IN VIRGINIA. SHE VISITED
ENGLAND WITH HER HUSBAND IN 1616, WAS GRACIOUSLY
RECEIVED BY QUEEN ANNE WIFE OF JAMES I.
IN THE TWENTY SECOND YEAR OF HER AGE SHE DIED
AT GRAVESEND, ENGLAND WHILE PREPARING TO
REVISIT HER NATIVE COUNTRY, AND WAS BURIED
THERE, IN ST. GEORGE'S CHURCH ON MARCH 21ST 1617.

A plaque dedicated to Pocahontas was given by the Washington Branch of the APVA in 1915. Her image is from a portrait at Sedgeford Hall, the Rolfe ancestral home in England.

A plaque in memory of the Colonial Governors and Presidents of the Council was given by the Society of Colonial Dames of America in the State of Virginia.

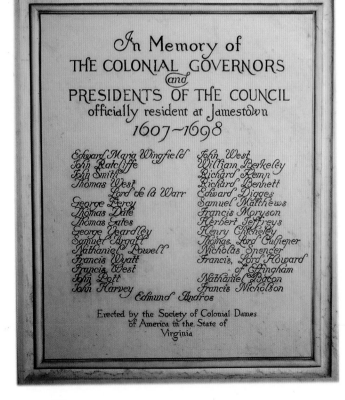

In Memory of
THE COLONIAL GOVERNORS
and
PRESIDENTS OF THE COUNCIL
officially resident at Jamestown
1607–1698

Edward Maria Wingfield   John West
John Ratcliffe   William Berkeley
John Smith   Richard Kemp
Thomas West   Richard Bennett
    Lord de la Warr   Edward Digges
George Percy   Samuel Matthews
Thomas Dale   Francis Moryson
Thomas Gates   Herbert Jeffreys
George Yeardley   Henry Chicheley
Samuel Argall   Thomas, Lord Culpeper
Nathaniel Powell   Nicholas Spencer
Francis Wyatt   Francis, Lord Howard
Francis West   of Effingham
John Pott   Nathaniel Bacon
John Harvey   Francis Nicholson
        Edmund Andros

Erected by the Society of Colonial Dames
of America in the State of
Virginia

The Graveyard

Tombstones were rare in colonial Virginia due to the scarcity of natural stone in the Tidewater region. They would have been an indicator of family wealth, since they would have most likely been imported from England. Unfortunately, many tombstones in the Jamestown Church graveyard were lost, stolen or destroyed by the ravages of time.

Of the twenty-two granite tombstones marking the graves in the Jamestown Church graveyard, many have inscriptions that are still legible. Additionally, there are inscriptions marking the tombs inside the Church. The inscriptions which follow, using the spelling and punctuation of the time, offer historical insight into early colonial life.

The Reverend James Blair (1656–1743): (translated from Latin) "Here lies buried the reverend and honorable James Blair, A.M. Born in Scotland, educated in the University of Edinburgh, he came first to England then to Virginia in which part of the world he filled the offices for 58 years, of preacher and gospel, for 54 years of Commissary, of president of William and Mary, of a Councillor to the British governors, of President of the Council and of Governor of the colony. The comliness of a handsome face adorned him. He entertained elegantly in a cheerful, hospitable manner, without luxury. Most munificently he bestowed charity upon all needy persons. In affability he excelled. He had a well varied library founded for the College. Dying, he bequeathed his own library by will for the purpose of informing students in Theology and instructing the poorer youth. He departed this life the 14th day before the calends of May (April 18th) 1743 at the age of 88. Works more lasting than marble will commend to his the nephews the surpassing praise of a well beloved old man."

Mrs. Sarah Blair (1670–1713): "Memorum Sacrum (In sacred memory) Here lies in the hope of a blessed resurrection the body of Mrs. Sarah Blair, wife of Mr. James Blair, Commissary of Virginia, sometime minister of the parish. She was daughter of Benjamin and Mrs. Hannah Harrison of Surry. Born August the 14th, 1670, married June the 2nd, 1687. Died May the 5th, 1713, exceedingly beloved and lamented." There follows a long Latin inscription (now lost) attesting to her virtues.

Mrs. Hannah Ludwell (1678–1731): "Under this stone lies interred the body of Mrs. Hannah Ludwell, relict of the Honorable Phillip Ludwell, Esq. by whom she has left one son and two daughters. After the most exemplary life spent in cheerful innocence and the continual exercise of piety, charity and hospitality, she patiently submitted to death on the 4th day of April, 1731 in the 52nd year of her age."

William Lee (1739–1795) and William Ludwell Lee (1775–1803): "In memory of Honorable William Lee, son of Col. Thomas Lee and Hannah Ludwell his wife. He was born at Stratford Hall, Westmoreland County, Virginia, August 31st, 1739 and died at Greenspring, James City County, Virginia, June 27th, 1795. He was the only American ever elected an Alderman of London where he also served as sheriff. He sacrificed these honors and a large mercantile business to follow the fortunes of his native country in the struggle for independence.
ALSO
William Ludwell Lee son of William Lee and Hannah Phillipa Ludwell his wife. He was born at London, January 23rd, 1775 and died at Greenspring, January 24th, 1803.

Phillip Ludwell (1672–1726): "Here lies interred the body of Phillip Ludwell who died the 11th of January 1726 in the 54th year of his age, sometime an auditor of his Majesties revenue and twenty-five years a member of the Council."

Mrs. Ursula Beverly (1681–1698): "Here lieth interred the body of Ursula Beverly, late wife of Robert Beverly, and daughter of the very honorable William Byrd, who departed this life the 11th day of October, 1698, being much lamented by all that knew her, aged 16 years, 11 months and 2 dayes."

John Clough (?–1684): "Here lyeth interred the body of the Rev. John Clough, late minister of this place, who departed this life January 15, 1683–4 and waits in hope of a joyful resurrection." (Clough is buried inside the Jamestown Church.)

There are other tombstones with only fragments of decipherable inscriptions. These include stones for an Elizabeth Drummond and Lady Frances Colpeper Stephens Berkeley, the wife of Governor Sir William Berkeley. The grave of Benjamin Harrison I, (?1645–1649) reportedly had three bodies in it, a practice typical in England at the time. Other people are said to be buried here, but the locations of their graves and tombstones have been lost. They include: Edward Ambler (1732–1767); Mary Cary Ambler (?–1781) wife of Edward Ambler; Jacquelin Ambler (1742–1797); Edward Jacquelin (?–1730); Phillip Ludwell of Greenspring; and Sarah Grymes Ludwell, wife of Phillip Ludwell.

There are twenty–two granite tombstones marking the graves in the graveyard beside the Jamestown Church.

Captain John Smith Statue

Captain John Smith (1580–1631) was a soldier and adventurer. By the time the first group of settlers arrived in Virginia, Smith was in chains, accused of mutiny. However, a sealed box with orders from the Virginia Company contained names of seven individuals who were to be members of the council that was to govern the colony. When the box was opened, Smith's name was on the list. In 1608, Smith was elected president of the governing council and the settlement grew under his strong leadership. He enforced order and a strict work policy including an edict that "he that will not worke, shall not eate." He made improvements to the fort, explored the region, and traded with the Powhatans for food. However, a gunpowder injury forced Smith to return to England in 1609.

Smith is remembered as one of the first American heroes. His leadership in the early years of Jamestown saved the Colony. But he is also remembered through his extensive writings about Virginia.

The bronze statue of Captain John Smith stands just south of the church, his gaze forever fixed on the James River which brought him to Jamestown. Smith holds a book in his right hand, representing his writings about Virginia. His left hand rests on his sword. The inscription on the base of the statue reads: "Captain John Smith, Governor of Virginia 1608."

The statue was sculpted by William Couper of Norfolk and New York City. It was donated by Joseph Bryan, the newspaper publisher, and his wife Isobel and unveiled by their grandson Joseph Bryan III on May 13, 1909.

Pocahontas Statue

Standing north of the Jamestown Church, not far from the statue of John Smith, is the statue of Pocahontas. Born around 1595, Pocahontas was the favorite daughter of Powhatan, the ruler of the Powhatan Confederacy. Her birthplace, Werowocomoco, was 16 miles from Jamestown. Smith believed she saved his life twice during the colony's first years. From 1608 to 1609 she was a frequent and welcome visitor to Jamestown, often bringing gifts of food from her father.

Pocahontas married English tobacco planter John Rolfe in April, 1614. Their marriage helped to establish peaceful relations between the Indians and the English. In 1616, she visited England with her husband and infant son, Thomas. Pocahontas died on March 21, 1617 while en route back to Virginia. She was buried in St. George's Church in Gravesend, England where an identical statue stands.

Despite the fact that Pocahontas was highly revered by the ladies of the APVA, it took quite a few years for her statue to be placed at Jamestown. The statue of Pocahontas that now stands at Historic Jamestowne was created by William Ordway Partridge. It depicts a romanticized twentieth-century image of Pocahontas dressed in Plains Indian-style clothing and originally stood at the 1907 Jamestown Tercentennial Exposition in Norfolk, Virginia. The statue was moved to Jamestown in 1922. Participants in the dedication ceremony included descendants of Pocahontas and John Rolfe.

Myths and Legends of The Jamestown Church: Pocahontas' Wedding

Legend has long held that Pocahontas and John Rolfe were married at the Jamestown Church. In reality, the facts suggest that they were probably married in the nearby settlement of Henricus.

Pocahontas and Rolfe met while Pocahontas was being held captive by the English. She had been kidnapped in 1613 by Samuel Argall, who demanded a ransom from her father, Powhatan, in exchange for her return. While being held at Henricus, Pocahontas converted to Christianity and took the name Rebecca. She and Rolfe were married, probably at the church in Henricus, on April 5, 1614.

The most famous image of the wedding of Pocahontas is Henry Bruekner's 1855 painting *The Marriage of Pocahontas.* It depicts a scene more fanciful than truthful. The clothing is romanticized, the building is far grander than the church in either Jamestown or Henricus, and there are more English women depicted in the painting than were in the whole of Virginia in 1614!

MARRIAGE OF POCAHONTAS TO JOHN ROLFE   1857-29

Postcard circa 1915–1930 depicting a version of Henry Brueckner's painting The Marriage of Pocahontas.

The Memorial Gates

The large wrought iron gates that stand near the Jamestown Church were given by the Colonial Dames of America. They originally demarcated the boundary of the APVA grounds. Today they provide a picturesque reminder of Jamestown's early twentieth-century history.

Steamers large and small and river craft of all kinds resting on the bosom of the placid waters, giving life and color to the scene... When the boats arrived, both flying the American and British flags, a procession was soon formed which passed through the stately gates and on by the restored Memorial Church to the platform which was already surrounded by a dense crowd and shaded by the ancient trees facing the Tower which marks the spot of the venerable Church.

–Mrs. J. Taylor Ellyson, President, APVA,
describing the events of May 13, 1907

Chapter Four
Remembering Jamestown

Historic Celebrations

For generations, Americans have traced their heritage back to Jamestown. Ever since the American Revolution, gatherings have been held at Jamestown to mark each siginificant anniversary. Here Americans gather to celebrate, commemorate, and remember our beginnings as a nation.

The first documented celebration of the founding of Jamestown took place in 1807. The Jamestown Jubilee, as the 1807 event was called, attracted up to 3,000 people who converged at the crumbling ruins of the old church tower. The grand procession included the Bishop of Virginia, James Madison, who was second cousin to soon-to-be-elected President James Madison. Accompanying him were the residents of Jamestown Island as well as citizens of Norfolk, Williamsburg, James City County, a marching band and an artillery company. According to the periodical the *Virginia Argus,* the venerable Bishop of Virginia, elevated on one of the oldest tombs in the churchyard, "poured forth his pious soul in rendering grateful thanks to the great author of nature, and for the blessings which we enjoy."

This penny postcard shows visitors in front of the church tower. The postcard was published by I. Stern, New York about 1907–1915, but the wooden shed adjacent to the tower, identifies the image as earlier.
APVA Preservation Virginia collection

Visitors at old Church ruins, Jamestown, Va.

In 1857, just before the Civil War broke out, another Jamestown celebration took place, marking 250 years since the colonists landed. Attendance was estimated at 6,000 to 8,000 people. Sixteen steamships, bedecked in flags and streamers, were anchored in the James River. Former President John Tyler was the guest orator, holding forth for two and a half hours.

A contingent of visitors from Philadelphia wrote about visiting the old church tower:

We strolled up the vine covered ruins and crumbling graves of the old church and churchyard. As is well known, all that remains of Jamestown is a portion of the tower and walls of the old church and a brick magazine, now used as a barn. The strength of these buildings preserved them from the total destruction which befell the city in 1676. The graves are much mutilated—less indeed by the lapses of time, which has touched these hallowing memorials with a gentle hand, than by the ruthless curiosity of man.

The article in the *Virginia Argus* noted that the governor sent guards to surround the graveyard and prevent festival visitors from taking pieces of tombstones as souvenirs of the event.

Postcard showing the visiting congressional committee appointed to arrange the 1907 celebrations of the 300ᵗʰ anniversary of the settlement of Jamestown.
APVA Preservation Virginia collection

Jamestown became a popular sightseeing destination during the late nineteenth century. Here a group gathers around the church tower, probably on Jamstown Day, the anniversary of the arrival of the first settlers at Jamestown, ca. 1900.

There was no formal preservation movement in Virginia at the time of the first two Jamestown celebrations. The old church tower and graveyard were considered something of a romantic ruin. Citizens lamented the general deterioration and vandalism, but no one knew quite what to do. The Civil War and its aftermath effectively deterred any preservation efforts for decades.

However, by the time of the 300th anniversary of Jamestown in 1907, many things had changed. The Virginia economy had rebounded somewhat. Transportation was easier and excursions by train or boat were a popular pass time. A renewed interest in Virginia's colonial history had sprung up and interest in historic sites throughout the Commonwealth and across the nation grew dramatically. Recognizing that attention would be closely focused on them during the anniversary year, the leaders of the APVA worked hard to ensure that they were ready.

Plans were made on a grand scale for May 13, 1907. The main focus of the statewide celebration was the Jamestown Tercentennial Exposition in Norfolk, which was open from April to November, 1907. The Exposition was similar to a World's Fair and featured historical and technological exhibits along with a midway and other entertainment.

Many visitors also made the pilgrimage to Jamestown itself and the new Memorial Church in Jamestown, erected to mark the 300th anniversary, would play a key role in the festivities there.

The National Society of Colonial Dames of America formally presented the church to the APVA on May 11, 1907. Visitors from all over the United States traveled to Jamestown for the occasion. A choir of 50 choristers "clad in snowy vestments" sang the processional hymn "O God of Bethel." Mr. Joseph Bryan accepted the building on behalf of the APVA and Dr. Thomas Nelson Page delivered the main address. Several commemorative plaques were unveiled in the church that day.

Earlier that week, May 9, 1907 the Colonial Dames of America had made a gift of the wrought iron Memorial Gates to the APVA. At that ceremony Mr. J. Alston Cabell, representing the Dames, praised the work of the ladies of the APVA. He said, in part, "To them now belongs the honor of rescuing from the ravages of the flood this Island of Jamestown; this birthplace of the nation; this gateway of the greatest country the sun ever shone upon."

On May 13, 1907, the Memorial Church served as a key site for the ceremonies of the Tercentennial. After the opening prayer by Bishop A. M. Randolph, many patriotic addresses were made, including remarks by Governor Claude Swanson and the Honorable James Bryce, the British Ambassador to the United States.

The Memorial Gates were presented to the APVA by the Colonial Dames of America.

Mrs. J. Taylor Ellyson, president of the APVA from 1910-1935, eloquently described the event in an entry to the association's minute books dated January 4, 1908.

> *Steamers large and small and river craft of all kinds resting on the bosom of the placid waters, giving life and color to the scene... When the boats arrived, both flying the American and British flags, a procession was soon formed which passed through the stately gates and on by the restored Memorial Church to the platform which was already surrounded by a dense crowd and shaded by the ancient trees facing the Tower which marks the spot of the venerable Church.*

For many years the APVA ran expeditions known as "pilgrimages" to Jamestown aboard steamers like the Brandon and the Pocahontas.

Ticket.
APVA Preservation Virginia collection

A. P. V. A.
EXCURSION TO JAMESTOWN
STEAMER BRANDON
The Three Hundredth Anniversary of the Landing of the first Colonists at Jamestown.
MAY 13th, 1607   MAY 13th, 1907
Steamer Leaves Wharf at 8.00 A. M.
ROUND TRIP, $1.00.

COUPON.
Retain this coupon and present when boarding the BRANDON at Jamestown.

The 350th anniversary of Jamestown in 1957 was marked by many improvements at Jamestown. Although scholars at the time believed that the site of the 1607 fort had been lost to shoreline erosion, excavations at the site of the later New Towne settlement shed new light on everyday life in mid seventeenth-century Virginia. To celebrate the anniversary year the Commonwealth of Virginia created Jamestown Festival Park (now the Jamestown Settlement), complete with recreations of the three ships, the James Fort, and a Powhatan Indian village.

A variety of special events also marked the year. On May 13, the traditional date of the settlers' landing at Jamestown, Vice President Richard Nixon was the guest speaker. On May 23, the Descendants of the Barons of Runnymede presented a silver paten to the Jamestown Church. The Virginia Daughters of the American Revolution gave a "holy table" on June 14. During the annual Governors' Conference in Williamsburg, the governors of 47 states came to the Church for a communion service. On July 30, 1957 there was a celebration of the anniversary of the first convening of the General Assembly in the Church.

President Franklin Delano Roosevelt visiting the Jamestown Church on July 5, 1936.

Queen Elizabeth II visited Jamestown on October 17, 1957. She attended a brief prayer service at the Jamestown Memorial Church and requested that Sam Robinson (shown on the right) tell his story about the Mother-in-Law tree.

Unquestionably, the highlight of the year was the visit to the Church by Queen Elizabeth and Prince Philip on October 17, 1957. Escorted by Governor Stanley, the royal couple attended a brief prayer service in the Church. A replica of the silver communion chalice and paten used in 1662 was presented to the Queen.

The Queen Mother at the statue of Captain John Smith in 1954. Photo courtesy of Rodney Taylor

Just as the discoveries a century ago during Mary Jeffery Galt's excavations of the church fueled the excitement surrounding the 1907 celebration, the recent findings of the Jamestown Rediscovery® archaeological project have focused the international spotlight on Jamestown once again, just in time for the 400th anniversary commemoration in 2007.

Recent findings of the Jamestown Rediscovery® archaeological project have focused the international spotlight on Jamestown once again, just in time for the 400th anniversary commemoration in 2007.

At the center of Historic Jamestowne, the Jamestown Church stands as an enduring symbol of secular and spiritual importance. Its cobblestone foundations, so carefully preserved under glass, are representative of the foundation of America itself. Its old tower, the only structure from the seventeenth century that survives above ground at Historic Jamestowne, evokes with quiet dignity the solidity of the colonists' faith and determination to prevail in this new land. It is equally a living legacy of the ardent preservationists who were determined to claim Virginia's rightful place in American history. Over the years it has attracted the attention of politicians, royalty, and celebrities and in the process it has captured the attention of Americans of all races, religions, and backgrounds.

Vice President Al Gore visiting the Jamestown Church on April 24, 1993. Photograph courtesy of Ann Berry

Virginia Governor Tim Kaine (seated in center) and his cabinet visited the Jamestown Memorial Church on May 11, 2006.
Photograph by Michaele White

Vice President Dick Cheney, left, is joined by Virginia House of Delegates speaker, William Howell during a commemorative session of the Virginia General Assembly in Historic Jamestowne's Memorial Church, January 2007. The session was part of the commemoration of the 400th anniversary of the founding of Jamestown. Virginia's General Assembly, the nation's oldest continuously meeting legislative body, first began meeting in the Jamestown Church in July 1619.
Photograph by Steve Helber. AP/Wide World Photos

Artists throughout the years have been inspired by the Jamestown church. Above is a 1931 woodblock print entitled "The Church at Jamestown" by J. J. Lankes; below is a later drawing of the church by Nancy C. Witt of Ashland, Virginia
APVA Preservation Virginia collection

SOUVENIRS

Since the late nineteenth century, Jamestown has been a popular tourist destination. Naturally, visitors wanted a memento and there have been many souvenirs produced over the years depicting the Jamestown Church. A selection of postcards from the APVA Preservation Virginia collection is shown here to illustrate the variety of these early images.

At right: Although the postcard at right bears a few factual errors, it shows an iconic view of the church tower and memorial church. Published by H. D. Cole, Newsdealer, Williamsburg, VA, circa 1915–1930.

Below: There was more text than photograph on this postcard, which urged visitors to "See First Things First." Attracting some of the thousands of Williamsburg tourists to nearby Jamestown to see where Virginia history began has been a goal. Published by the APVA, circa 1940.

Old Church, Built in 1640. Jamestown Island, Virginia. The site of the first permanent English settlement in America. May 13, 1607. It is undoubtedly the most interesting of all historic places in the United States. Here was the seat of government in Virginia from 1607 to 1698. Here the Princess Pocahontas was baptized in the Christian faith and married to John Rolfe.

THE OLD CHURCH TOWER

See First Things First

Only 7 miles from Williamsburg is

Jamestown Island

The first Permanent English Settlement in America
1607-1698

"Of all historic shrines, the most impressive."

Here Sir Walter Ralegh's dream of colonization at last came true, and English civilization in America was established; here amid famine, massacre, war and pestilence, the soul of the Nation was born.

Within the grounds of the ASSOCIATION FOR THE PRESERVATION OF VIRGINIA ANTIQUITIES the lover of beauty and of history will alike find complete satisfaction and experience a thrill felt nowhere else.

Come and see these hallowed grounds in their present beauty enshrined in a glorious past. Open 8 A. M. until sunset.

ADMISSION 25 CENTS

Take a breezy 15-minute trip on the Jamestown Ferry to Smith's Fort Plantation and all points south.

Within the image:
JAMESTOWN MEMORIAL
CHURCH. Built in 1907. The
third brick church erected at
Jamestown. The TOWER ruin is
a relic of the first brick church
of 1639-47, which was burned in
Bacon's Rebellion.

Glossy black and white postcard describes the Jamestown Memorial Church. Published by DOPS, circa 1925–1942.

Black and white postcard showing the eroded riverbank near the old church tower where graves were revealed. It had a postmark of May 13, 1957, the date of the 350th anniversary of the founding of the colony. Published by the APVA, around 1950.

This postcard of the Memorial Church has a rather morbid caption on the back. It describes the old sycamore tree (the so-called Mother-in-Law Tree) which "sprung up between the tombs of Commissary Blair and his wife and dismembered them." Published by the APVA, circa 1910–1930.

A painting by William J. Paxton for the Life Insurance Company of Virginia was reproduced for this postcard of the Jamestown Church. Published by the Life Insurance Company of Virginia, circa 1930–1960.

THE CHURCH AT JAMESTOWN, VIRGINIA

Penny postcard shows the church tower with the barbed wire fence that was put up to deter relic hunters from scavenging the ruins. Published by the Hugh C. Leighton Company, Portland, Maine, circa 1907.

Old Church Tower, Jamestown, Va.

Black and white postcard showing some of the old tombstones in the church graveyard. Published by an unknown publisher, circa 1905.

Romanticized illustration shows Pocahontas and Captain John Smith, the church tower and the fort. The layout of the fort is known to be much different today than shown here. The postcard is a souvenir of the Jamestown Exposition of 1907 and is typical of the souvenirs produced for the Exposition, many of which were not overly burdened by historical accuracy. Published by A. C. Bosselman & Co., New York., circa 1907.

Souvenir of the Jamestown Exposition of 1907. Copyright by J. G. McCrorey & Co. Baltimore Badge & Novelty Co., Lith., 1906.

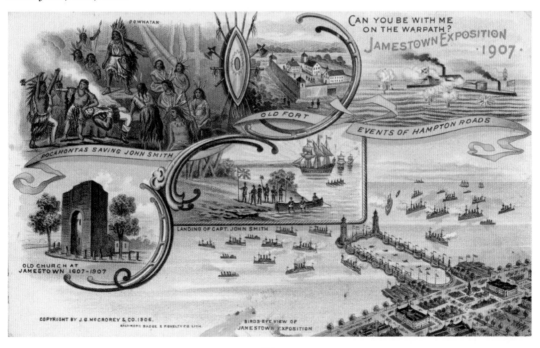

Text on the back of this hand colored postcard reads: "Burned during Bacon's Rebellion, the old church tower still stands at the entrance. The Brick house of worship, erected after the Bacon uprising was used until 1758. On the walls of the present structure are memorial tablets commemorating 'the adventure in England and the ancient plantation in Virginia,' the Jamestown Colonial Governors, Bruton Parish Church and the famous characters: Capt. John Smith, Pocahontas, Chanco, Rolfe, Lord Delaware, Claiborne, Daniel Gookin." Published by B. E. Steel, Jamestown Island, VA, circa 1930-1945.

This postcard image shows the church tower with a wooden shed behind it. The shed had been built to protect the excavations of the church in the late nineteenth and early twentieth centuries. Copyright by Detroit Photography, 1902.

6243. OLD CHURCH AT JAMESTOWN, VA.

COPYRIGHT, 1902, BY DETROIT PHOTOGRAPHIC CO.

In addition to postcards, a variety of other souvenirs have been produced over the years for sale to tourists. Many of these feature the church, an enduring symbol of Historic Jamestowne. What follows is a selection of souvenir items from the APVA Preservation Virginia collection bearing images of the church.

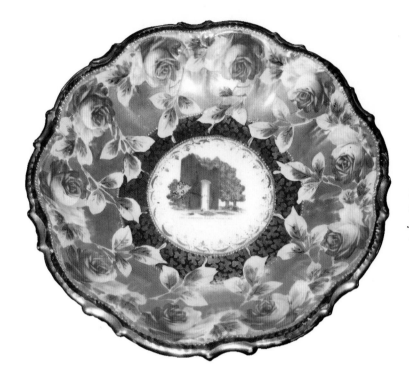

This hand painted porcelain bowl with gilt details depicts the Jamestown Church and is dated 1907.

Earthenware plates with transfer printed decorations, like this plate that depicts Pocahontas, John Smith, the three ships, and the Jamestown Church, were common souvenirs in the early years of the twentieth century. Similar items are still being manufactured today.

Ceramic plates with flow blue decoration, like this one depicting the Jamestown Exposition and local tourist sites including the Jamestown Church, were extremely popular during the late nineteenth and early twentieth century.

This ribbon dates to about 1895 and is probably a souvenir of an early pilgrimage to Jamestown.

Silver commemorative spoons were popular souvenirs around the turn of the twentieth century. This one depicts the "Ruins of Jamestown" on the bowl.

The teacup, toothpick holder, and spoon rest, all souvenirs of the 1957 Jamestown Festival, are decorated with colorful decals that show the Jamestown Church.

From the Virginia Company's instructions to the Settlers (1606):

"Lastly and chiefly the way to prosper and achieve good success is to make yourselves all of one mind for the good of your country and your own, and to serve and fear God the Giver of all Goodness, for every plantation which our Heavenly Father hath not planted shall be rooted out."

Suggested Reading

A Land As God Made It: Jamestown and the Birth of America, by James P. P. Horn: Basic Books, 2006.

Holy Things and Profane: Anglican Parish Churches in Colonial Virginia, by Dell Upton: Yale University Press, 1997.

Images of America: Jamestown, by Rodney Taylor and William Molineux: Arcadia Publishing, 2004.

Jamestown, An American Legacy, by Martha McCartney: Eastern National, 2001.

Jamestown and the Founding of the Nation, by Warren M. Billings: Thomas Publications, 1991.

Jamestown Rediscovery 1994–2004, by William M. Kelso and Beverly Straube: APVA Preservation Virginia, 1994.

Jamestown, The Buried Truth, by William M. Kelso: University of Virginia Press, 2006.

Jamestowne Ancestors 1607–1699, by Virginia L. H. Davis: Genealogical Publishing Co., 2006.

Visit us on-line for information about Historic Jamestowne, the Jamestown Rediscovery® archaeological project, educational resources, the Jamestown Biographies Project genealogical data-base or to shop for books, educational games, reproductions, videos, jewelry and so much more.

www.historicjamestowne.org